ST IVES GUIDE

by

Peter Stanier

Acknowledgements.

The publisher is most grateful to St Ives Town Council, particularly for the
assistance of the Town Clerk Mr Malcolm Veal, for providing details of
civic ceremonies and allowing the St Ives Borough crest to be illustrated in
the Guide. To the Hon. Curator of St Ives Museum, Mr Brian Stevens for
casting his expert eye over the manuscript and his advice and to local
photographers Mr Stephen Bassett, Mr Richard Clegg and Mr Tony Smith
for their generous contributions.

St Ives Guide

© **Peter Stanier**

Individual contributors retain all rights to their photographs
and intellectual property.

First Edition published April 2004

Designed and Typeset by Tobi Carver

Photography & illustration: Tobi Carver

Maps by Nick Griffiths

Additional Photography: Toni Carver, Stephen Bassett,
Richard Clegg & Tony Smith

Printed & Published by:
The St Ives Printing & Publishing Company,
High Street, St Ives, Cornwall TR26 IRS, UK.

ISBN 0 948385 36 7

CONTENTS

GETTING TO ST IVES

By road: Turning off the A30 at St Erth, take the A3074 through Lelant and Carbis Bay to St Ives; alternatively, before Lelant follow the detour route via Lelant Downs Road to join the B3311 from Penzance near Halsetown and enter St Ives from the west. The main car park is above the town at Trenwith Burrows, alongside the Leisure Centre and Swimming Pool, but there are others at Ayr, Barnoon and the railway station. There are less accessible parks at Porthmeor Beach, The Island and Carncrows, the Sloop, and on Smeaton's Pier, but driving through the town is a continuous nightmare as all the streets are congested. A guide book of the 1930s stated: 'The streets of St Ives are so narrow and so busy that the motorist should inquire whether he will be in order in leaving his car by the kerb for more than a minute or so.' Just try doing that today! The town is also served by coach and bus services for those without a car.

By rail: St Ives is connected by branch line to St Erth station which has main line services to Penzance and the rest of the country. For motorists, a frequent park-and-ride railway service runs from Lelant Saltings. This is a very good way to visit St Ives on a day trip, by avoiding parking problems while at the same time you can enjoy the scenic line along the cliffs. There are tantalising glimpses of your destination as St Ives and the harbour get closer all the way.

The St Ives Tourist Information Office is situated in the Guildhall, Street-an-Pol, where visitors will find details about the town, its surroundings, accommodation and much more. The TIC can also be contacted on 01736 796297

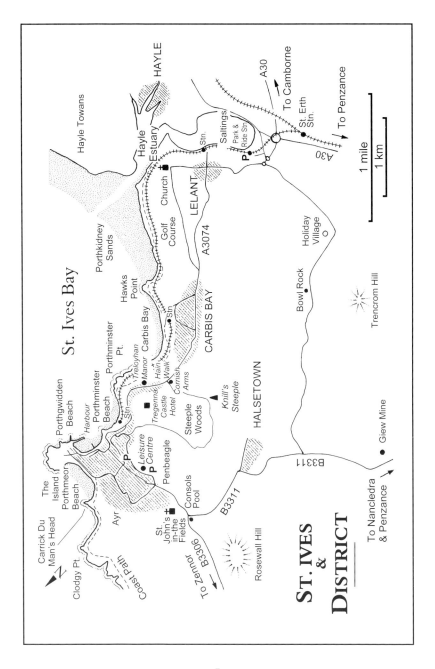

St. Ives Bay

ST. IVES & DISTRICT

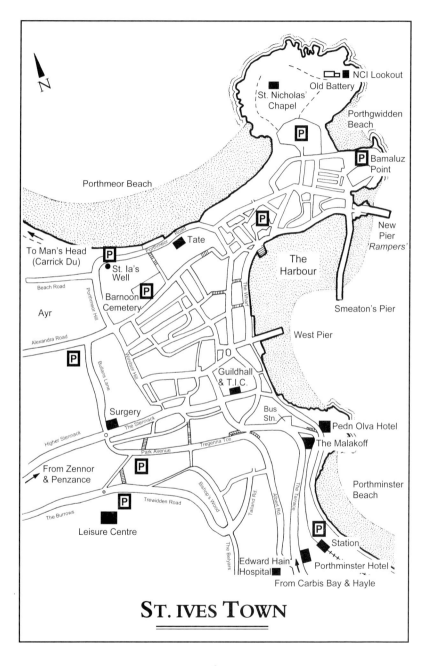

N

NCI Lookout
Old Battery
St. Nicholas' Chapel
Porthgwidden Beach
P
Bamaluz Point
Porthmeor Beach
New Pier
'Rampers'
Tate
To Man's Head (Carrick Du)
The Harbour
St. Ia's Well
Beach Road
Barnoon Cemetery
Ayr
Smeaton's Pier
Alexandra Road
West Pier
P
Guildhall & T.I.C.
Surgery
Bus Stn.
Pedn Olva Hotel
The Malakoff
Higher Stennack
Park Avenue
From Zennor & Penzance
Porthminster Beach
Trewidden Road
The Burrows
Leisure Centre
Station
Edward Hain Hospital
Porthminster Hotel
From Carbis Bay & Hayle

St. Ives Town

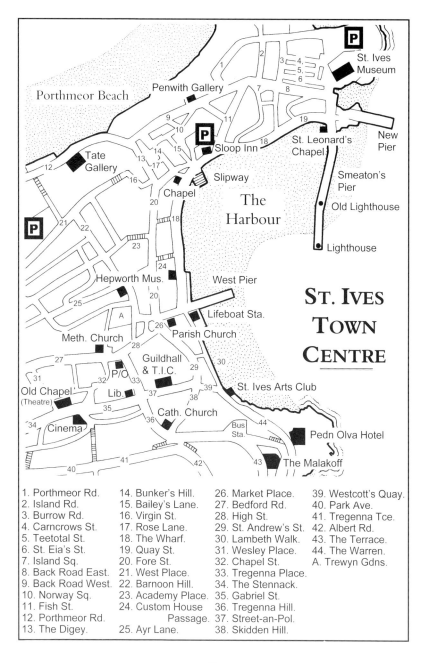

St. Ives Museum

Porthmeor Beach

Penwith Gallery

New Pier

St. Leonard's Chapel

Sloop Inn

Tate Gallery

Slipway

Smeaton's Pier

Chapel

The Harbour

Old Lighthouse

Lighthouse

Hepworth Mus.

West Pier

Lifeboat Sta.

Meth. Church

Parish Church

Guildhall & T.I.C.

P/O

Old Chapel (Theatre)

Lib.

St. Ives Arts Club

Cinema

Cath. Church

Bus Sta.

Pedn Olva Hotel

The Malakoff

ST. IVES TOWN CENTRE

1. Porthmeor Rd.	14. Bunker's Hill.	26. Market Place.	39. Westcott's Quay.
2. Island Rd.	15. Bailey's Lane.	27. Bedford Rd.	40. Park Ave.
3. Burrow Rd.	16. Virgin St.	28. High St.	41. Tregenna Tce.
4. Carncrows St.	17. Rose Lane.	29. St. Andrew's St.	42. Albert Rd.
5. Teetotal St.	18. The Wharf.	30. Lambeth Walk.	43. The Terrace.
6. St. Eia's St.	19. Quay St.	31. Wesley Place.	44. The Warren.
7. Island Sq.	20. Fore St.	32. Chapel St.	A. Trewyn Gdns.
8. Back Road East.	21. West Place.	33. Tregenna Place.	
9. Back Road West.	22. Barnoon Hill.	34. The Stennack.	
10. Norway Sq.	23. Academy Place.	35. Gabriel St.	
11. Fish St.	24. Custom House	36. Tregenna Hill.	
12. Porthmeor Rd.	Passage.	37. Street-an-Pol.	
13. The Digey.	25. Ayr Lane.	38. Skidden Hill.	

Looking towards Smeaton's Pier, the lighthouses and a packed Porthminster Beach

One of the many B&B's in St Ives   *Bethesda Hill*

WELCOME TO ST IVES

The old fishing port of St Ives is one of the best known gems of the Cornish coast and few visitors fail to be attracted by the resort's many charms. Its location could hardly be bettered, at the same time both dramatic and picturesque, set by a rocky headland at the edge of the wide sweeping bay to which it gives its name. The old town of pretty stone cottages clusters around a harbour filled with colourful fishing craft sheltered behind a pier with its own lighthouse, and there are beaches of golden sand for surfing and bathing. Mellow local granite stone is found throughout this idyllic place, in the houses, the pier, paving and streets. Wild moorland hills of granite provide a perfect backdrop just behind the town. St Ives enjoys a mild climate, being partly surrounded by the sea and influenced by the Gulf Stream; there are seldom frosts and snow is a rarity so that semi-tropical plants can be grown with some success. This does not mean however, that the town escapes from extremes of weather, from the ravages of storm force winds or inundating floods to hot balmy summer days when the blue ocean is flat and tranquil. It is small wonder then that this spot has become frequented by tourists and artists.

Unique charm

St Ives has still managed to retain its character despite the influence of tourism, which makes the town one of Cornwall's favourite destinations, whether for a day visit or as a place to stay a while. What is there for the visitor to see in this small place? There are beaches for bathing, surfing or just relaxing, the harbour, restaurants, galleries, souvenir shops, surfing shops, churches, interesting architecture, the lifeboat, the museum and local walks. Places of interest in the neighbourhood are within easy reach by foot or car, while local coach tours operate in the summer to many other Cornish towns and attractions. St Ives is well served with hotels, guest houses and self-catering

9

accommodation and the population of around 10,000 more than doubles during the summer months.

St Ives is famous for its gulls and its cats and even the names of the narrow streets and ways are part of the town's rich heritage, like Bethesda Hill, The Digey, Virgin Street, Court Cocking, Fish Street, Salubrious Place or Teetotal Street. The common prefix 'Chy' in place names, such as Chy-an-Gweal, means 'house'. Visitors are greeted with well maintained floral displays around the town, for the council gardeners are proud of their many successes in the annual Britain in Bloom contests. The small community boasts a surprising number of local customs and events throughout the year and the town retains its own independent weekly newspaper, *The St Ives Times & Echo*.

This small guide provides an introduction to St Ives and its many points of interest.

Fishing boats, St Ives harbour

Porthminster Beach, the Harbour and The Island

A SHORT HISTORY

It is likely that the rocky promontory of Pendinas, now called The Island, was a defensive fort in prehistoric times. Later, the early settlement developed on the low neck of ground joining The Island to the mainland, with Porthmeor Beach on one side and the more sheltered harbour on the other. According to legend the Irish missionary St Ia or Eia sailed onto the shore below Pendinas (where she was given sanctuary) on a leaf in the early 5th century. She was sister a of St Euny and St Erth, and gave her name to Porthia, the old name for St Ives.

St. Ives was to become an important trading port with a pilchard fishery as well as a mining community. The town was dependent on the church at Lelant several miles away until 1434 when its own church was dedicated. A market charter of 1490 indicates that the place was of some importance and it was around this time that a first small pier was built and a light was lit on The Island to guide sailors at night. During the rebellion of 1497, Perkin Warbeck is said to have landed nearby when claiming the throne as Richard IV, although he is also said to have landed elsewhere in Cornwall. St Ives was involved in the Prayer Book Rebellion of 1549 when Cornishmen protested at the loss of the Latin prayer book. When the rebellion was suppressed the town portreeve John Payne was invited to have gallows erected in the Market Place while he was entertaining the Provost Marshal Sir Anthony Kingston to lunch. Afterwards, Payne was duly hanged by Kingston for his involvement in this Catholic protest. In 1558 St Ives became a Parliamentary Borough, returning two members to parliament until the Reform Act of 1832. It remains a constituency for a single MP today.

The borough gained a mayor in 1639 and in the following year a silver Loving Cup was presented by Sir Francis Basset of Tehidy and this still forms part of the annual Mayor Choosing ceremony in May. Even the Civil War of the 1640s was felt in St. Ives, which was otherwise a long way from the main action. Here, unlike much of the rest of Cornwall which was fiercely Royalist, St Ives stood out for Parliament but this outrage was put down briefly by Sir Richard Grenville for the King. Plague followed in 1647.

Mining was developing in the neighbourhood all this time and there are late-16th century records of shipments of copper ore to smelters in South Wales. Tin was also worked and shipped off. By the 1720s Daniel Defoe described St Ives as 'a pretty good town and grown rich by the fishing trade.' St Ives was at the forefront of the growing Methodist movement, being visited many

The 'Old Customs House'

times by John Wesley between 1743-89. The harbour was greatly improved for shipping and the fishing fleet by the building of Smeaton's Pier in 1767-70. The most famous Customs Officer at this time was John Knill, who is remembered by a curious ceremony held every five years. The Customs Port of St Ives, where sailing ships and fishing boats were registered, extended along the coast to St Agnes, but Hayle became important enough in the boom years of the mining trade to have its own customs house in 1864-82.

The beach of the tidal harbour once came right up to the houses erected along its shore and boat building took place here until the mid-19th century. Much activity was concerned with fishing, when ships brought salt or barrel staves from the Baltic and others sailed with cargoes of salted and barrelled pilchards for the Mediterranean market.

Coal was also imported (the last ship called at the pier in 1935) and sailing boats traded with limestone from South Wales and Plymouth for burning in lime kilns which stood near the site of the Museum. A few walls in this area contain limestone blocks, bearing witness to this industry.

Pilchard seining was important throughout the 19th century, as was drift netting for mackerel and herring. From 1840 onwards the port has been served well by successive generations of lifeboat crews. The pier was extended in 1890 and the West Pier was built four years later. The town spread out onto the higher ground above the old heart with the building of terraces of new houses in the late 19th and early 20th centuries.

Probably the greatest industry at St Ives has been tourism. The opening of the railway branch line in 1877 gave rise to the tourist industry which began to blossom at a time when the fisheries were starting to fail. There was a brief interruption in the Second World War, during which time a Commando cliff-training unit was based at St Ives for training in the area. The establishment of an artists' colony during the 1880s alongside the fisheries and growing tourism grew into one of the best known aspects of the town. Many famous names were part of the 'St Ives School' which became internationally renowned and the successful St Ives Tate Gallery at Porthmeor recognises this importance.

The Tate Gallery

Granite detail

Greenstone, or blue elvan, detail

Raised beach and 'head' deposit, Porthmeor

GEOLOGY

Although many of its houses are built of local granite, much of St Ives actually stands on another rock, greenstone. This is a hard dark igneous rock, difficult to work for building, and exposures can be seen for example on The Island, Carncrows and Man's Head, where there is an old quarry at Carrick Du. It was once molten, like the slightly younger granite which was intruded about 290 million years ago, baking the greenstone close to the contact. The granite is exposed further inland, such as on Rosewall Hill which is topped with rounded tor formations. Granite is the rock of the West Penwith peninsula and is characterised by large white or brownish crystals of feldspar inter-spersed with glassy quartz and shiny mica. You only have to stand next to a wall in St Ives to see the attractive qualities of this crystalline rock.

Copper and tin minerals in near-vertical lodes or veins are found all around St Ives and were mined from shafts or adits (tunnels) for centuries. An unusual form of huge ore body found locally was a 'carbona', and the Great Carbona was worked out in a massive cavern in the St Ives Consols Mine. The Trenwith Mine was briefly famous for pitchblende, a source of uranium.

Younger geology mostly relates to changes in sea level over time. Beyond St Ives, the shelf between the granite hills and the sea cliffs seen from the coast road to Zennor and St Just would seem to represent an old shoreline from perhaps as late as 12 million years ago. Even more recent are 'raised beaches' containing fossilised beach pebbles and sand visible in sections of cliff just above the high tide level at The Island and on the west side of Porthmeor. One of the best in the district, though, is to be seen in the cliff at Godrevy on the far side of St Ives Bay. Sea level was once lower too. Peat deposits found in the foundations for the new lifeboat house confirmed that there was once land here and that sea level has been rising steadily since the Ice Age. The 'earthy' cliffs around Porthmeor also contain 'head', a mixture of brownish earth and jum-bled rock fragments, formed during the Ice Age when the area was subjected to perma-frost conditions. Of more immediate date are the great dunes of blown beach sand, best seen at Lelant and the extensive Hayle Towans. Finally, just take away the houses of St Ives in your imagination and you will see a low sandy spit between the mainland and The Island, vulnerable to frequent breaching by winter storms.

Rounded granite formation at Trencrom Hill, similar to those found on hills at Zennor and Rosewall

WILDLIFE

Herring Gull

Resident flocks of herring gulls are always about the town, nesting on rooftops and scavenging the harbour area and beaches to plague pasty-eating tourists in the summer. Black-backed gulls are also seen, along with turnstones and oyster catchers along the water's edge. The Island is a popular location for bird watching, where gannets make a fine display on stormy days, skimming the wave crests and plunging for fish.

Grey Seal

Cormorants, shags and terns are common too. The Island is also a good place from which to spot dolphins, porpoises, basking sharks and even small whales which sometimes come into the bay. The bizarre sunfish is also seen from here on occasions. Seals are fairly common along the coast and sometimes come into the harbour itself.

Shag

Basking Shark

The Sloop Inn, circa 1312

BEACHES

All the beaches at St Ives feature clean golden sand. Porthmeor Beach is on a beautiful bay between The Island and Man's Head where it faces the full Atlantic swell, making it the town's principal surfing beach. A surf school is based here and a number of surf shops in the town will also hire out wetsuits and boards. The scene is overlooked by a café, the Tate Gallery, artists' studios and flats. The much smaller Porthgwidden Beach lies between The Island and Bamalûz Point, where it is open to St Ives Bay. It feels much more 'private' than the other beaches and can be sheltered when it is windy over at Porthmeor. It was once a fishing cove. Even the harbour has a golden beach at low tide, but beyond is Porthminster Beach which takes its name from a chapel or 'minster' sited here until the early 15th century. In more recent times numerous seine fishing boats were drawn up above the high tide mark but now the beach is a place to relax and enjoy its safe bathing. Facilities include beach huts and the Porthminster Restaurant. Around the headland to the south is another popular bathing beach at Carbis Bay.

Late summer football on Porthgwidden beach

Love Lane

Victoria Road

The Market Place

AROUND THE TOWN

O ne of the great pleasures of St Ives is that you can wander at will, exploring its small streets and alleys, many of which give glimpses of the harbour; or you can contemplate the scene from all sorts of viewpoints. It is impossible to get lost, for nowhere is far away. Down'long is the true old part of St Ives on the low land between The Island and the mainland, with the harbour on one side and Porthmeor Beach on the other. This was the fishermen's quarter but today many cottages are second homes or holiday lets. Upalong is the higher part of the town developed in the later 19th century and it was here that the sea captains, tin miners and professional classes made their homes. A number of the larger houses have become guesthouse accommodation. To locals there is a clear distinction between these two parts of town.

The Tourist Information Centre is in the Guildhall, but the best starting point for a tour on foot is in the Market Place where the Parish Church with its great tower dominates all. All traffic from the High Street to The Wharf and Fore Street has to navigate the Market House in front of the church. This rounded building dates from 1832 when it replaced a much earlier one from 1490. It was the home of the Borough Council until it moved to the new Guildhall in 1940. Also in the Market Place, at the corner of High Street and St Andrew's Street, the War Memorial is an impressive Celtic cross carved in Cornish granite and set in a small garden.

The St Ives War Memorial stands guard over the entrance to the Memorial Gardens

The circa 1831 'old' lighthouse (foreground) looking towards the 'new' lighthouse first lit on 29th September 1890

THE HARBOUR

Just below the church are the West Pier and lifeboat station. West Pier dates from 1894, and it is hard to believe that roadstone from the local greenstone quarries was shipped from here for a time. Despite its commercial origins, the *St Ives Weekly Summary* soon reported that West Pier had become 'quite a fashionable promenade.'

A walk around the harbour along The Wharf starts at the lifeboat house by West Pier. Designed by local architects Poynton Bradbury Wynter, this granite building under a slate roof was completed in 1994 in order to accommodate the new 12-metre Mersey class lifeboat *The Princess Royal* for which purpose a new slipway was also built in front. Previously, the lifeboat was towed on its carriage all the way along The Wharf to the slipway by the Sloop Inn. A visit to the lifeboat house is always popular with visitors, who can inspect the lifeboat and learn of the many past rescue missions. A wall plaque outside commemorates the loss of seven of an eight-man lifeboat crew in the disaster of 23rd January 1939, while set in the ground is a millstone salvaged from the SS *Nile*, lost on The Stones on 30th November 1854. It was this wreck that finally led to the building of the Godrevy lighthouse. On the opposite corner of the road the old lifeboat house of 1867 was converted into the 'Alba' café and restaurant in 2002. Beside this is the austere granite frontage of the Salvation Army Citadel.

Before the road along The Wharf road was widened behind a sea wall in 1922, the sandy harbour beach came right up to the houses along the shore. There are other points of interest along here, despite the many restaurants, shops and amusement arcade. Just past the Lifeboat Inn, the Old Customs House has bay-fronted windows on the first floor. Next to it Customs House Passage provides a narrow link with Fore Street. Woolworth's is the most incongruous building here, standing on the site of Paynter's boatyard. A little further on Court Cocking is a second narrow link to Fore Street. Cocking family members have served on the lifeboat for generations. The back of the Fore Street Methodist chapel dominates the far end of The Wharf. Facing the old lifeboat slip, the Sloop Inn is said to date from 1312 and is the sole survivor of at least four public houses along The Wharf. Also known as 'the artists' pub', where artists met and some paid in kind, the bar walls were hung with paintings by local artists and caricatures by Harry Rowntree. When the public bar was enlarged in 1954 the landlord commissioned Hyman Segal to produce portraits of his locals.

Three fishermen's lodges standing between the road and the harbour are much treasured establishments where retired and working fishermen meet and socialise. The Wharf narrows further along. Beside the United Fisherman's Co-op look out for the Ship Aground, dated c1650. The way narrows again into Quay Street, before emerging at the pier. Just here is the tiny St Leonard's Chapel, once a fishermen's chapel, later a store and now containing a few fishing exhibits and a bronze memorial which lists the names of 61 fishermen lost from St Ives between 1833 and 1940.

St Leonard's Chapel

Smeaton's Pier shelters the boats in the harbour, although only the first part was designed by the celebrated civil engineer. John Smeaton, having successfully completed his Eddystone Lighthouse, was invited to design a pier for St Ives, which was duly built with large granite blocks at a cost of £10,000 in 1767-70. Look out for a small bronze memorial on the pier's sea wall recording the artist Harry Rowntree, 1878-1950. A New Zealander, he was a Fleet Street caricaturist who continued his work in St Ives. A lighthouse was erected perhaps as late as 1831 on the end of Smeaton's original pier and was soon after lit by gas supplied from the new town gasworks. A low granite structure with a domed top, it became redundant when the pier was extended in 1890 and was used as a store for a while. It was burnt out in an arson attack in 1996 and a new dome and lantern were designed for its restoration.

The Victoria Pier extension was completed in 1890 and you can see the change in alignment and in the granite stonework. Note also the Roman numerals up to 'XX' carved in the granite stonework to indicate the depth of water in feet at the landing steps. Near the end a memorial states that the foundation stone was laid by T. Bedford Bolitho, MP, on 25th June 1888, with the final stone being placed two years later to the day by Edward Hain, JP and mayor. The contractors were Thomas Lang & Sons, who also built the floating dock at

An eye-catching iron bollard

Penzance. The white pierhead lighthouse is of iron, manufactured by Stothert & Pitt Ltd of Bath (later known for dock cranes erected at most major ports) and its fixed light was first lit on 29th September 1890. The eight bollards on the Victoria extension are made of shaped granite for mooring shipping and fishing boats. Elsewhere on the pier and around the harbour there are bollards of circular iron pipes with flanged tops. These were once used for pumping water from the depths of the local mines, and when those were closed down the redundant pipes found a new function here and at a number of other Cornish harbours.

The arches under the landward end of Smeaton's Pier were put in at the time of the Victoria extension to prevent sand accumulating in the harbour, but the current was so strong that it not only swept away the sand but also small boats as well! The arches were therefore partially blocked with timber baulks.

A Royal Commission of 1858 recommended that St Ives should become a harbour of refuge and the New or Wood Pier was built in 1864-5 in an attempt to make an outer harbour and give Smeaton's Pier more protection. This very exposed timber and stone pier only survived about two decades, but a granite wall survives and the foundations and timber piles (known as 'The Rampers') are still clearly visible at low tide. In stormy conditions the ruins of the pier provide a popular if potentially dangerous 'break' for surfers. From here it is not far to the Museum at Wheal Dream, from where a walk around Bamalûz Point leads to Porthgwidden Beach and The Island.

Deck chairs along the harbour front

THE ISLAND

The craggy island of Pendinas (derived from 'Pedn Enys' = Head Island) was once connected to the mainland by a strand, upon which are now built the houses of Down'long. There are traces of a small prehistoric fort around its summit. In 1538 John Leland noted a 'pharos for lighte for shippes sailing by night in these quarters' erected out on the head. St Nicholas' Chapel, on the west summit, was no doubt a daymark for shipping and is dedicated to a patron saint of seafarers. The original chapel was almost completely demolished in 1904 by the War Office who had been using it as a store. But a public outcry forced them to stop and Sir Edward Hain financed its rebuilding in its present form in 1911 to commemorate the coronation of King George V. The chapel was last restored in 1971 through the help of J.F. Holman. It is a focus for walkers and provides fine views over the town and both shores.

At the east end of The Island the old Battery has three circular Victorian gun emplacements, intended to protect the harbour and Porthmeor beach from enemy landings. Three 64-pounder guns were installed here in 1887, but were decommissioned eight years later. The building here was the gunners' quarters. On the very headland, the easternmost gun emplacement later became the foundation for a coastguard lookout. After closure by the Coastguard service, the lookout has been manned since August 1999 by members of the National Coastwatch Institution.

St Nicholas' Chapel

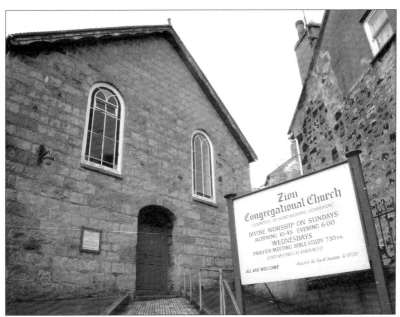

Zion Congregational Church, Salubrious Place, Fore Street

One of the many courtyards off The Digey

FORE STREET AND DOWN'LONG

L eading away from the church in the Market Place, Fore Street is paved with granite setts throughout its length, as is the case of many other lanes in Down'long. This is still the busiest shopping thoroughfare, although mostly catering for the tourist trade. It is really too narrow for traffic, but is always busy with pedestrians in the summer, seeking souvenirs, paintings in the galleries, pasties, restaurants or surf clothing and gear – all are catered for. There are narrow exits from Fore Street down to The Wharf by Customs House Passage and Court Cocking, while on the uphill side are the steep steps of Academy Place, with Virgin Street, The Digey and Bunkers Hill all worth exploring. Along Fore Street, the Zion Congregational Church (Countess of Huntingdon's Connexion) dating from 1800 is found in Salubrious Place. Next, are John Knill's house (he of the curious celebrations described later in the guide) and Cyril Noall Square, named after a great local historian and author of many books on the town, fishing, seafaring and mining. He died in 1984.

Virgin Street is a narrow and charming ascent to Barnoon Hill and the car park, while The Digey is the most convenient way through to Porthmeor. A granite archway in Hicks's Court just off The Digey

The Digey

29

marks the site of the dwelling of George Hicks who was portreeve in 1611 and 1624. The Fore Street Methodist Chapel, built in 1831 as a Primitive Methodist Chapel, stands between the street and The Wharf. Its Sunday School is opposite, just up Bunkers Hill at the corner of Rose Lane. Fore Street now emerges onto The Wharf from which Fish Street, Bethesda Hill and other narrow ways lead into the residential part of Down'long, where can be found Island Square and St Eia, Teetotal and Carncrows Streets. Pudding Bag Lane, often spotted in old photographs, was a typical Down'long street which was demolished to make way for the Sloop car park and craft market. The Island, Porthgwidden Beach and the Museum are all hereabouts.

Along Back Road West, the humble frontage of the Bible Christian Chapel (1854) is opposite the Penwith Gallery. There follow the Porthmeor artists' studios and then a group of cottages known as Harry's Court where the primitive artist Alfred Wallis lived. Look for the small plaque 'Alfred Wallis, Artist and Mariner 1855-1942'. The Digey leads back to Fore Street, but it is no distance around the corner where the road opens out on Porthmeor Beach and the sea, overlooked by the Tate Gallery and Barnoon cemetery. St Ia's Well (Venton Ia) is at the foot of Porthmeor Hill below the cemetery. A climb up the steps beyond the Tate to the Barnoon car park gives a fine view over the beach, before returning to the Market Place by a descent of Barnoon Hill. This passes Dame Barbara Hepworth's old studio and the Wills Lane Gallery right at the bottom of the hill.

Barnoon Cemetery

30

HIGH STREET TO TREGENNA

The High Street leads into the Market Place as the main road into the old town. Here are 19th-century banks and the post office on the corner of Tregenna Place and Bedford Road. Boots the chemist was formerly the Scala Cinema, hence its architecture. This was the site of the stables for the Queens Hotel (opposite), which was the coaching inn of the town. The narrow alley on the left is called Sugar Lane and leads to Street-an-Pol and the Guildhall, past the offices and shop of the local newspaper. The United Methodist Church dominates the end of Bedford Road and nearby is the entrance to the Trewyn Sub-Tropical Gardens, lovingly cared for despite frequent attacks of vandalism which never seem to stop the town's gardeners being consistent winners in the Britain in Bloom competition.

The Library at the corner of Tregenna Place and Gabriel Street was donated in 1896 by J. Passmore Edwards, the Cornish philanthropist who gave many libraries and institutions for the good and education of the poor throughout his native county. The Archive Centre, based on the first floor of the Parish Rooms in St. Andrew's Street, has facilities for researching many aspects of St Ives and the area. Opposite the Library is Street-an-Pol, where visitors will find the Tourist Information Centre in the Guildhall which was built in 1939-40. Outside is Dame Barbara Hepworth's bronze sculpture 'Dual Form', presented in 1968. Hepworth and the potter Bernard Leach were both made Freemen of the Borough of St Ives. A crossroads at the end of Street-an-Pol meets Skidden Hill, an old way into the town, and St Andrew's Street which leads back to the church. An early customs house is here and the lane continues to Westcott's Quay where the St Ives Arts Club has its weather-boarded headquarters. The promenade back to the lifeboat house and West Pier is popularly known as Lambeth Walk, although its official name is Pedn

Barbara Hepworth's Dual Form

Olva Walk. In the other direction, The Warren is a narrow lane to Porthminster Beach and the railway station, with the Pedn Olva Hotel at the corner.

From the library, Tregenna Hill begins the long climb out of town towards Carbis Bay. The Catholic church of the Sacred Heart and St Ia was built in 1909 on the first corner. A wall plaque commemorates the events of the Prayer Book Rebellion of 1549 and the townsmen who died in defence of the Catholic faith, including the portreeve John Payne who was hanged in the Market Place by Sir Anthony Kingston. Around the corner in Fernlea Terrace is the house of James Halse, one time mayor and MP for St Ives, now Chellews, the solicitors. Further on, The Malakoff takes its name from the fort of the Crimean War and provides a good viewpoint over St Ives and the harbour from above a high wall. Barbara Hepworth's bronze sculpture 'Epidaurous' is here. Down below is the car park formed from the old railway station yard. The main road continues up past The Terrace, where the Rt Hon George Devereux De Vere, Earl of Essex, lived at No.27 in 1810-34. Further up Trelyon Avenue are two of the town's largest hotels, the St Ives Bay and Porthminster Hotels, and around the next bend can be seen the former Coastguard cottages alongside the hill.

Tregenna Castle Hotel commands the whole scene from high above. This was built for John Stephens in 1774 to the designs of John Wood the younger, the well known architect of Georgian Bath. The Great Western Railway turned it into a hotel and despite many extensions it retains its castellations. The parkland grounds have staggering views of the bay and there is a golf course here too.

Pedn Olva Hotel and Point

UPALONG

Back at Library Corner (a popular place for traffic jams), Gabriel Street leads into Royal Square, which has the Western Hotel and Royal Cinema (built 1939). Chapel Street leads back to Bedford Road and the High Street. The Stennack is the long hill bringing the road into St Ives from the west. The partly covered stream down the valley here is prone to overflowing and flooding parts of the town, notoriously in November 2002 when shops in Tregenna Place found themselves under several feet of water and the inshore lifeboat saw action in the street! The former Wesleyan Chapel has been converted into the St Ives Theatre for the enthusiastic Kidz R Us Theatre Group. Founded in 1994, this successful band of youngsters has performed to acclaim at venues as varied as the Albert Hall in London or the open air Minack Theatre on the Cornish cliffs at Porthcurno. Next door, the granite-faced Wesleyan School of 1845 ('AD MDCCCXLV') is a back-packers' hostel. Around the back in Street-an-Garrow was the home of John Nance where John Wesley stayed on several of his visits to St Ives from the 1740s onwards.

Further up the hill, the Stennack Board School of 1881, later a Junior School, was saved from a threatened demolition when it became the doctors' surgery and pharmacy. The old hamlets of Trenwith (mentioned in Domesday Book) and Hellesvean have now been engulfed by St Ives. Up here, St Johns in the Fields church was built in the late 1850's and consecrated in 1860 to the design of J.P. St Aubyn, a prominent church architect of the day. In the fork of the road at the very top of the hill is Consols Pool which once supplied water to the St Ives Consols Mine. Model boats are traditionally sailed here every Good Friday morning.

Overlooking the Stennack Valley and the town is the main car park at Trenwith Burrows, where the St Ives Leisure Centre has a 25-metre pool, a children's pool, gym and café. These facilities resulted from a long and successful local campaign.

The Parish Church tower and the carved Lantern Cross

THE PARISH CHURCH

S t Ives church is dedicated to St Ia as well as Saints Peter and Andrew. Legend has it that St Ia landed here in the fifth century, having sailed from Ireland on a leaf, which must be an interpretation of the skin boats in use during the Dark Ages and of a type still seen today in the curraghs of the western Irish coasts. St Ia was supposed to sail with other saints but got left behind. Such was her determination to set out on her missionary work that she was able to use the miraculous leaf! Her Feast Day is 3rd February.

This lovely church standing on the edge of the shore is a haven of peace amid the summertime bustle. It was built in 1410-34 when great granite blocks were used in the construction, including the tower which

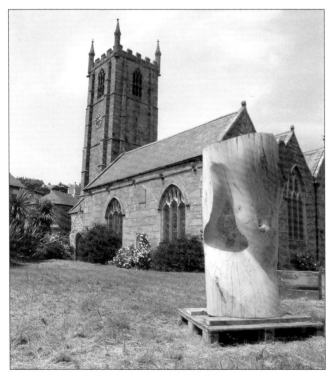

St Ives Parish Church

is over 80 feet (24 metres) high. The stone is said to have been brought from the cliffs near Zennor, which seems an extremely hazardous operation when there were plenty of granite 'moorstones' lying freely on the hills close to St Ives. If the story is true, this must reflect the dire condition of the roads and tracks around the town. Unusually, the arcade piers are made of an imported freestone. Off the south aisle is the Lady Chapel, or Trenwith Aisle. There is a brass to Oto Treunwyth (1463) and his wife, and Barbara Hepworth's stone carving 'Madonna and Child' which is in memory of her son killed on service in the RAF in 1953. The 15th-century granite font is presumably original. Of a similar date there is some carved wood in the choir stalls, including one depicting a blacksmith's tools. The wagon roofs, typically Cornish, have carved angels.

Outside the church is a lantern cross on an octagonal shaft, about 10 feet (3 metres) high. It was rediscovered in the 19th century and re-erected in 1852. The four sides have carvings showing Christ on the cross, the Madonna and child, a bishop and possibly St Ia. The church-yard was once much larger and what remains is protected from the sea by a wall.

A detail of one of the engraved pews at
St Ives Parish Church

36

ST IVES MUSEUM

St Ives Museum was founded by the Old Cornwall Society in 1924 and has been housed in the old Seamen's Institute Mission at Wheal Dream since 1968. It is among the most interesting town museums in Cornwall, packed with displays about the history of St Ives and the neighbourhood, from prehistoric stone axes to more familiar household artefacts of the 20th century. The museum also covers many aspects of fishing, mining, agriculture, railways, wrecks and the lifeboat. The theme of the sea is ever present and there are instruments from the Longships and Pendeen lighthouses, while the Hain Room has fine models and other items of the Hain Steamship Co., established in St Ives in 1878. The bell of the *Trewidden* is here, the firm's last merchant ship sold off in 1974. The museum is administered by trustees and volunteers – please give generously when you visit!

The St Ives Museum, formerly the Seamen's Mission.

Some scenes from St Ives' fishing heyday. Above fishermen repair their nets aboard some of the St Ives fleets two masted luggers. Below fishing vessels around Smeatons Pier

Photos: St Ives Times & Echo *collection*

FISHING

In 1750 there was a considerable trade in pilchards which were barrelled and sent to Spain and Portugal. Towards the end of that century one visitor described how all the inhabitants lent a hand when there was a large haul of fish but, on the minus side, he mentioned rather depressingly that 'the stench arising from the stores, and from the putrid "rejectamenta" lying about the town, is to strangers almost intolerable.' By the 1830s and '40s an average of 22 million pilchards were shipped every year to Italian markets, while herring and mackerel were sent to Bristol for home consumption.

The St Ives coast had 285 seining companies in 1870. The seine boats took out long seine nets to enclose a shoal of pilchards. Drawn in, the seething mass of fish was scooped out with baskets into smaller boats which took them ashore where the pilchards were pressed and salted in fish palaces or cellars. Any oil was collected and sold. September 1905 saw one of the greatest catches ever recorded at St Ives. An estimated 13 million pilchards were captured by the five seines shot in the bay and it took a week to empty them. Fish (and their smell) were everywhere and everyone who was available lent a hand in landing and processing this valuable catch during a week of intense excitement.

A huer's lookout still stands by the footpath on Porthminster Point at the start of Hain Walk. This is where the huer signalled directions to the seiners seeking the large pilchard shoals that came into the bay beneath. The cry of 'hevva' ('found') was accompanied by directions given by hand-held signals known as 'bushes'.

St Ives also had 186 lug-sailed driving boats in 1870 and the fleet of two-masted luggers sailed out beyond the bay to catch pilchards, mackerel and herring with drift nets. Their dark brown sails were a familiar sight but many were converted to motor boats between the two world wars. It was common to see the fishing nets laid out to dry on the grass of The Island. The open air fish market was held at the slipway near the Sloop Inn. Two large paintings by Edward King illustrating seine fishing and the fish market can be found in the Guildhall (please ask to view them).

Today, the smaller fishing boats in the harbour include hand-liners (often seen working off The Island when the tide is flowing) and crabbers. The *Dolly Pentreath* is a modern fishing lugger built to a traditional design and often takes visitors out to sea on sailing and fishing trips. Other boats will take you on a coastal cruise to Seal Island, or for sea fishing expeditions. There are also small boats for hire during the summer.

A view of St Ives Harbour and its current fleet

PILOT GIGS

Pilot gig racing has become a popular Cornish sport since the 1980s and the two St Ives gigs *Porthminster* and *Defiance* are kept at Carbis Bay. They can be seen being rowed across the bay during training sessions as well as races against other Cornish crews. Hayle also has two gigs. In the 19th century these long boats were rowed (and sailed) out to sea to put a pilot on board ships approaching the Bristol and English Channels. There was always competition among the gig crews, for whoever got their pilot to a ship first landed the contract.

40

THE LIFEBOAT

There has been a lifeboat at St Ives since 1840, although the RNLI did not provide a boat until 1861. Over the years over 1,000 lives have been saved and many more aided by the crews of a succession of boats powered by oars, sail and motor. Today's lifeboat *The Princess Royal* is a Mersey class boat, launched by trolley and tractor from a purpose-built house at West Pier, opened in 1994. A smaller inflatable inshore rescue craft has been stationed at St Ives since 1968. Visitors may see a launching (listen out for the firing of warning maroons) for a practice or a real mission when the lifeboat may be called out at all hours and in all weathers for search and rescue, to take off an injured crewman, or to stand by a crippled ship. On Lifeboat Day in August the lifeboat takes part in a display with a rescue helicopter off the harbour.

The old lifeboat house, which was too small for the new boat, later became a restaurant named the 'Alba' after a dramatic shipwreck at St Ives. On 31st January 1938 the steamship *Alba* was wrecked at the east end of Porthmeor Beach. In a rescue witnessed by many on the shore, the St Ives motor lifeboat *Caroline Parsons* took off her crew but

St Ives RNLI's Mersey Class lifeboat The Princess Royal

capsized, losing five of the sailors. A greater tragedy took place almost exactly a year later, on 23rd January 1939. The 3,000-ton steamship *Wilston* was reported in trouble down the coast in a force 10 north-westerly storm, and was subsequently lost with all her crew at Pendeen. It was impossible to launch the Sennen lifeboat and so the brave St Ives men went out at 3am. Their lifeboat soon capsized off Clodgy Point and was carried by the storm across the bay, capsizing at least twice more before being thrown up onto the rocks at Godrevy Point. Seven crewmen died and there was only one survivor. Their memorial can be seen on the wall of the lifeboat house. Visit the lifeboat and the popular souvenir shop.

Both St Ives' main and inshore boats regularly practice techniques with Royal Navy Search & Rescue Helicopters

THE HAIN STEAMSHIP CO.

Edward Hain & Sons built up a large fleet of tramp steamers that took general cargo whenever and wherever they were needed all around the world. The first Hain ship was a sailing brigantine in 1837, but the first of many steamships was the 1,800-ton *Trewidden*, built in 1878 by the Readhead yard at South Shields, from which over 80 more company ships were to be launched over the years. Characteristically, the names of all the Hain ships began with 'Tre-' and their black funnels bore a large white 'H'. The Hain Steamship Co. was formed by the fourth Edward Hain (later Sir) in 1901 by which date this successful shipping firm from tiny St Ives was the largest tramp steamer owner in Britain. Sir Edward Hain lost his son (also Edward) in the Great War, and after he died in 1917 the firm was bought by P & O who retained the name. The last ship (*Trewidden*) was sold from the fleet in 1974 and her bell is displayed in the museum.

The two world wars took a terrible toll on the Hain fleet, which lost 18 ships in the first conflict and an incredible 28 (out of 32) in the second. In peacetime there were shipwrecks, one famous one being the loss in 1923 of the *Trevessa* in the Indian Ocean, from which the surviving crew were obliged to sail for 1,500 miles in two open lifeboats. Three years earlier, the *Treveal* was wrecked nearer home on the Kimmeridge Ledges off the Dorset coast with the sad loss of 36 men. The Hain Room in the St Ives Museum is well worth a visit. Sir Edward Hain built Treloyhan Manor (now a Christian Holiday and Conference Centre). As a benefactor to the town, he repaired the St Nicholas Chapel on The Island and established the Edward Hain Memorial Hospital in memory of his son. His name is also commemorated by Hain Walk along the cliffs from Porthminster Point below Treloyhan Manor.

The Fairplay X *the last major grounding in St Ives Bay*   Photo: Toni Carver

The rarely seen sight of the Alba's *boilers and bow, covered in seaweed and only exposed at extreme low tides*   Photo: Stephen Bassett (Harbour Master)

SHIPWRECKS

Countless shipwrecks have occurred all along the inhospitable north Cornish coast and St Ives has had its own share too. The 'Cintra Gale' of November 1893 saw three remarkable wrecks next to each other on the beach at Carbis Bay. Three steam colliers, the *Cintra*, *Vulture* and *Bessie*, had come into St Ives Bay to shelter but when the wind strengthened and went round to the north-north-east they were driven onto the beach, where most of their crews were rescued by breeches-buoy. At the same time the SS *Rosedale* was driven onto Porthminster Beach, while 10 miles off Godrevy the SS *Hampshire* was lost in the same storm. There were still plenty of 20th-century wrecks around St Ives. In 1908 the three-masted sailing ships *Mary Barrow* and *Lizzie R. Wilke* were stranded on Porthminster Beach almost alongside each other. Both were outward bound from Swansea with coal, and although they were refloated only the former survived to sail for another 30 years. In January 1938 the 3,700-ton Panamanian ship *Alba* was on passage from Barry to Cintavecchia with coal when she was driven onto the rocks at The Island end of Porthmeor Beach and during the rescue the St Ives lifeboat was lost with five of the ship's crew. The *Alba*'s boiler is still visible at low tide close to the Island rocks. In 1952 HMS *Wave* was sheltering off the harbour when her anchors dragged and she was driven ashore at Westcott's Quay. Townsfolk came out to help rescue the crew. The naval ship, which was aground close up to the town, was later refloated.

Godrevy Lighthouse

GODREVY LIGHTHOUSE

This octagonal tower was completed in 1859 on a rocky island a quarter mile from the shore across the far side of St Ives Bay. It is a warning at the beginning of a mile-long line of viscous rocks, semi-submerged at high tide, known as The Stones; a buoy with a light marks the far seaward end. The Stones had caused a series of calamitous wrecks over the years. Between 1838 and 1858 there were at least 16 wrecks, although a few vessels managed to dislodge themselves and reach safety. Others, many unnamed, are only known from their wreckage found over the following days after they struck. One of the worst was the wreck of the steamship *Nile* on the 30th November 1854. Bound from Liverpool for Penzance, Plymouth and London, the 700-ton ship was lost with all hands (25 crew and about 10 passengers) and it was this wreck that led to the successful petitioning of Trinity House for a lighthouse.

Although it would have been much safer for mariners, a plan for a rock tower lighthouse at the end of The Stones was dismissed as being too expensive. Instead, the tower was built at a cost of £7,082 15s 7d on Godrevy Island in 1858-59 to the design of James Walker, the Trinity House engineer responsible for many famous lights including the Wolf Rock and the Needles. Workmen lived in tents on the exposed island while construction took place and a temporary lightship was stationed offshore. Even after Godrevy Lighthouse was first lit on 1st March 1859, there were still a few wrecks on The Stones. The first two were reckoned to be ships mistaking the new light for the Longships off Land's End! With the reduction in shipping coming to Hayle or St Ives, Trinity House planned to close the lighthouse in 1932 but after much local opposition it was redeemed but became automatic in 1934. The 86-foot tower stands 120 feet above high water and the light is visible for 12 miles. It has a flashing white light but there is a red sector which becomes visible when boats sail into the danger zone near The Stones. In rough seas, spray can be seen being driven right over the tower. The lighthouse across the bay is very much part of the scene viewed from St Ives and is the subject of Virginia Woolf's book *To the Lighthouse*.

The Mayor prepares to hurl the silver ball, one of the events during Feast Monday

St Ives' principal civic event, Mayor Choosing and the ceremonial sip from the Loving Cup

CUSTOMS AND EVENTS

For a small community it is surprising how many customs are upheld throughout the year, often blessed by the involvement of the mayor and town council. Visitors react with both surprise and pleasure when they happen to be in St Ives on the right day and stumble unawares upon one of its traditions.

Feast Day is the first Monday following the 3rd of February, which is St Ia's day when the church was consecrated. Children dance in procession through the streets to St Ia's Well (Venton Ia) at the foot of Porthmeor Hill, where the Silver Ball is blessed. Then, at 10.30am the silver hurling ball is thrown by the mayor from the churchyard wall to a crowd of waiting youngsters on the beach below. A mad scramble ensues and whoever returns the ball to the mayor at the Guildhall at noon receives a crown piece. Pennies are thrown to waiting children by councillors from the Guildhall balcony. The Western Hunt has usually left from Royal Square on Feast Day.

Mayor Choosing takes place in May and is the principal event in the town's civic calendar. The outgoing mayor gives thanks and a proposer commends the incoming mayor (chosen previously by the council) who gives a speech about their intentions for the year. Following the civic ceremony, the Loving Cup (presented by Sir Francis Basset in 1640) is taken outside the Guildhall where local school children queue to drink from it with the mayor and mayor's consort. The cup was originally to show that there was no discourse between councillors; today, the symbolism is more of the council serving the community. Saffron buns are also given to the children by the councillors. The mayor of St Ives is always addressed as Mr Mayor regardless of sex – a tradition vigorously upheld by the lady mayors!

Model boat sailing on Consols Pool takes place on Good Friday mornings when both young and old boys gather here to sail their model yachts. There was an old custom of seamen and fishermen placating the storm gods by launching model boats onto the sea. The town council ensures the pool is cleaned each year to assist the tradition which is attended by the mayor and councillors.

49

The Midsummer Eve Bonfire was revived by the St Ives Old Cornwall Society and takes place on Carnstabba Hill, where the mayor lights the fire. With echoes of a very ancient rite, flowers and herbs are thrown by the 'Lady of the Flowers' into the hilltop blaze. The gathering is blessed by the vicar and prayers are said in Cornish.

The John Knill Celebration is held every five years on St James' Day (25th July) when 10 girls in white with two widows, a fiddler, parson, customs officer and the mayor parade to Knill's Steeple on its hill high

Good Friday boating

The quinquennial John Knill Celebrations

above the town, where the girls dance around and the 100th psalm is sung. This is all in memory of John Knill (1733-1811), the one-time customs officer (and some say he was also a smuggler) who had the monument built above his intended mausoleum. He worked as a lawyer in London where he died and was buried at Holborne, but he left a legacy for this curious ceremony to be held ever since. Knill's iron chest is opened outside the Guildhall, and then the party proceeds via St Andrew's Street, the High Street and Tregenna Place to The Malakoff, where they are transported to Steeple Hill. Originally the widows and little girls were chosen from the families of miners or fishermen. John Knill's House is near Salubrious Place in Fore Street.

Crying the Neck is an ancient ceremony marking the end of the harvest which is carried on by the Old Cornwall Society on a local farm. The last sheaf of corn is cut and held aloft by the reaper who cries out 'I have 'ee,' onlookers then shout three times, 'What have 'ee,' to which the reaper replies, 'A neck, a neck, a neck.'

Crying the Neck

51

A two-week **September Festival** of music and arts has been held on and off since the 1970s, when dozens of top professional folk, blues, jazz and classical acts perform at venues throughout the town. Art exhibitions and open studio days are arranged and there are many talks and workshops staged, together with plays and shows from the local theatre groups.

New Year's Eve

Christmas and New Year is a time of celebrations. The Fair Mo, an ancient pig fair, is still held before Christmas. Around Christmas the 'Cock Robin Choir' traditionally sang the Cock Robin song outside the houses of those who had offended the community during the year, and created mischief around the town, with items sometimes being removed to most unusual places. Not surprisingly, few are unhappy that this custom has fallen off in recent years. A growing and popular event now takes place on New Year's Eve when the town comes alive with revellers in fancy dress, locals and visitors alike.

ARTISTS AT ST IVES

Although artists had visited St Ives before (J.M.W. Turner sketched the harbour in 1811), it was the opening of the railway in 1877 that brought the town to the wider attention of artists. Attracted by the scenery, and more importantly the clarity of the light, a 'colony' of artists grew rapidly in the 1880s. This was at a time when similar colonies were forming at Newlyn and Falmouth as well as in Europe and the USA. These artists sought a simple life where they could paint real scenes in the open air - part of a movement that spread across Europe from the USA. A number of artists visited St Ives, while others became resident here so that the colony soon had over 100 members. The St Ives Arts Club was founded in 1890 and its premises on Westcott's Quay is still the venue for concerts, poetry and musical evenings, art exhibitions and reviews. The Porthmeor studios were established in old fish cellars, helped by Julius Olsson. The first artists were treated with some suspicion in the tight-knit fishing community, and in this deeply religious society it was not wise to be found out painting on a Sunday!

Bernard Leach established a pottery studio at St Ives in 1920 with his friend Shoji Hamada, having studied ceramics in Japan for 11 years. This famous potter of international renown was a founder-member in 1927 of the St Ives Society of Artists, which now holds exhibitions in the former Mariners' Church (built 1906 in memory of Canon Jones of St Ives) in Norway Square. The avante guard painters Ben Nicholson and Christopher Wood first came to St Ives in 1928 when they discovered the 'primitive' painter Alfred Wallis (1855-1942), a retired seaman and store dealer who took up painting in his 70s, using just about any available scrap of board or card for his work. He died in poverty in Madron workhouse but his grave in the Barnoon cemetery is decorated with painted tiles depicting a lighthouse designed by Bernard Leach. The St Ives School of Painting was established by Leonard Fuller and his wife Marjorie Mostyn in 1938. Early pupils included Sir Terry Frost, Sven Berlin and Peter Lanyon. After Fuller's death in 1977 Roy Ray became the principal; the school is now managed by a board of trustees.

The sculptor Dame Barbara Hepworth was born in Wakefield in 1903 but lived and worked at St Ives from 1939 until her death in 1975.

She and her second husband Ben Nicholson first lived at Carbis Bay and were joined during the war years by other artists including the sculptor Naum Gabo. The late 1940s and 1950s were particularly fruitful years which brought national and international recognition to St Ives through the works of painters such as Ben Nicholson, Peter Lanyon, Patrick Heron, Wilhelmina Barns-Graham, John Wells, Terry Frost and Bryan Wynter, or the sculptors Barbara Hepworth, Sven Berlin and Denis Mitchell. There have been, of course, many others. Barbara Hepworth and Bernard Leach were given the Freedom of the Borough in 1968.

Alfred Wallis' house, Back Road West

GALLERIES

The Tate Gallery St Ives was opened in 1993, and is a stunning piece of modern architecture that fits perfectly within its surroundings where it overlooks the equally spectacular Porthmeor Beach. It was designed by Eldred Evans and David Shalev and rose from the derelict site of the town gasworks which had been established here in 1835. It was bombed in 1942, repaired the works continued in operation until the late 1950's, although for many years afterwards a gasholder stood here. Inside the gallery is a collection of modernistic paintings representative of the St Ives school and other parts of west Cornwall, with visiting exhibitions. Despite misgivings from some quarters, the gallery became a success almost overnight and was instrumental in drawing in new visitors and extending the holiday season at St Ives.

The Barbara Hepworth Museum and Sculpture Garden is in the famous sculptor's former studios at Barnoon Hill, where she worked from 1949 and later lived until her death in a fire in 1975. Her stone carving workshop is undisturbed and many sculptures in wood, stone and bronze can be viewed indoors and in the tranquil surroundings of the garden. Their forms relate to natural shapes in the landscape. Other examples of Dame Barbara's work can be seen around the town, in nearby Trewyn Gardens, outside the Guildhall, on The Malakoff and in the parish church.

The Penwith Gallery in Back Road West was once a fish cellar but is now the home of the Penwith Society of Arts, founded in 1949 by Ben Nicholson and Barbara Hepworth when the younger 'modern' artists broke away from the St Ives Society of Artists. Nearby are the Porthmeor Studios in lofts and former fish cellars, their windows giving a 'north light' as they overlook Porthmeor beach. They have been studios since the 1890s and

The Penwith Gallery

among the many famous artists to have worked here include Borlase Smart, Julius Olsson, Ben Nicholson, Patrick Heron, Tony O'Malley, Karl Weschke and many others.

The Mariners Gallery in Norway Square is the venue for exhibitions of work by the St Ives Society of Artists. This was the former Mariners' Church, built in the early 1900s in memory of Canon Jones of St Ives.

St Ives is packed with smaller galleries too numerous to list but among the older-established ones may be included the Salthouse Gallery, close by the Mariners Gallery, and the Wills Lane Gallery.

Wills Lane Gallery

WRITERS AND ST IVES

As with the artists, St Ives drew a group of writers here in the very early 20th century. Among them was Charles Marriott, who lived at Porthminster Terrace in 1903-10. The town was his 'Porthia', a hardly disguised name. Many years later he described the artists as 'a genial crowd, working reasonably hard and playing with zest - mostly golf at Lelant.' Among his acquaintances was Compton Mackenzie, who was then living at Phillack, Hayle. Mackenzie's first novel *Carnival* has a Cornish background, although his famous *Whisky Galore* was set in the Hebrides.

Edith Ellis, often known as Mrs Havelock Ellis (wife of Dr Henry Havelock, pioneer writer on the psychology of sex), lived in a mine count house at Carbis Bay, where she wrote *My Cornish Neighbours* in 1906. Here she converted miners' cottages into holiday homes. C. Ranger Gull (Guy Thorne) also lived here and his *Portalone* (1904) tells of artists in a fishing community surprisingly like St Ives! His friend A.G. Folliott-Stokes wrote of the little town of 'St Ars' and he devoted a whole chapter to St Ives in his book *The Cornish Coast and Moors*, where 'everybody and everything spells fish. Nothing else matters in St Ives. Nations may rise and fall, whole dynasties wiped out, but old St Ives cares for none of these things. Fish, or the absence of it, alone has power to quicken her pulse.'

The critic and biographer Sir Leslie Stephen bought Talland House in St Ives in 1881 and he was an early member of the Arts Club. His daughter Virginia Woolf spent childhood holidays here and, although the house was sold in 1896, she kept this memory alive and returned several times to the area in the early 20th century. Her famous novel *To the Lighthouse* was published in 1927. Seemingly set on the Isle of Skye, the family house and view across the bay are clear descriptions of St Ives, Godrevy Lighthouse and the bay across which the Ramsay family eventually set out to the 'stark tower on a bare rock.... the waves breaking in white splinters like smashed glass upon the rocks.' Talland House, in Talland Road, has been converted to flats.

The list of important St Ives writers of more recent years is endless but includes names such as the best-selling romantic novelist Mary Williams, Lelant-born Rosamund Pilcher whose books are based around St Ives and Cornwall (*The Shell Seekers* has been filmed), or Roy Phillips, author of *The Saffron Eaters*. Denys Val Baker came to live in St Ives after the Second World War and his many books include *Britain's Art Colony by the Sea* and *The Timeless Land: The Creative Spirit in Cornwall*. Sven Berlin, painter and sculptor, was notorious for his fictional portrayal of the St Ives art colony in *Dark Monarch*, a book withdrawn from sale after the publisher was served with three libel writs! Berlin's 'autosvenography' *Coat of Many Colours* included his St Ives years, war experiences and fishing. Hyman Segal also described his St Ives experiences, while local author Marion Whybrow has written on the St Ives artists (such as *St Ives 1883-1993 Portrait of an Art Colony* and *The Leach Legacy*).

Down the coast at Zennor, the naturalist-author W.H. Hudson spent the winter of 1906-7 in a cottage, a stay which resulted in his book *The Land's End*. It contains good accounts of contemporary life at St Ives, but Hudson did not endear himself to the townspeople of St Ives by writing of the ill-treatment of birds here. During the Great War, D.H. Lawrence and his German-born wife Frieda moved to Zennor in March 1916, staying at the Tinner's Arms before renting a group of cottages at Higher Tregerthen. He completed writing *Women in Love* here, although it was not published until later. The Lawrences were viewed with suspicion and the authorities gave them three days' notice to leave Cornwall in July 1917. Lawrence had been content here and recorded the time in a chapter in *Kangaroo* (1923). Helen Dunmore, a modern writer, brought Lawrence into her novel *Darkness at Zennor*. Lastly, Alison Symons' *Tremedda Days* is all about being raised on Tremedda Farm near Zennor and encountering the famous folk hereabouts.

CARBIS BAY

Carbis Bay, or Porthrepta, has a wide beach of golden sand providing safe sheltered bathing and a different kind of seaside holiday than its close neighbour St Ives. Visitors may care to walk the 1½ miles from St Ives along the pleasant coast path from Porthminster Beach. There is also a railway halt here, with a stone viaduct crossing the Carbis Valley nearby. There has been widespread housing development, particularly in the 20th century, so that Carbis Bay rivals St Ives in area. A hundred years ago there were far fewer houses and the land was scarred by old tin mine workings. Drainage levels (adits) emerge from the cliffs and collapsing shafts still cause alarm, while Count House Lane and Wheal Speed Road are place-name reminders of the historic industry.

January storm clouds over Carbis Bay beach

Lelant's St Uny Church

LELANT

The coast path continues beyond Carbis Bay to Lelant on the side of the Hayle estuary. There are golf links (the West Cornwall Golf Course is the oldest in the county) on the towans before reaching Lelant church. This was the mother church for St Ives until the town got its own church in 1434. Lelant's church is dedicated to St Uny, the brother of St Ia. By tradition there is a town buried beneath the sands here; even the church was threatened by encroaching wind-blown sand in more recent times. There are ancient wheel-headed crosses in the churchyard, while another is set on the war memorial on the way into the village. Return to St Ives by the path or take the train from Lelant station (its building is now a private house but trains stop at the platform). The park-and-ride scheme runs from Lelant Saltings. Few visitors driving through the village on their way to St Ives on the busy A3074 have time to turn off and explore Lelant.

Hayle from the Lelant side of the estuary, the final mooring for several of the area's fishing vessels

Early morning, Halsetown

The small farming village of Zennor lies five miles from St Ives

Halsetown

Halsetown lies just outside St Ives on the B3311 road to Gulval and Penzance. It has an interesting layout, having been a planned village financed by local solicitor James Halse (1769-1838), who was involved with the St Ives Consols Mine. He was also twice mayor as well as MP from 1826. The widely-spaced houses for miners were built in pairs with gardens. There was a school and at one time there were three chapels too. Halse built himself a town house in Fernlea Terrace, St Ives, in 1830.

Zennor

Five miles from St Ives along the winding B3306 coast road, this small granite village lies surrounded by tiny fields between a craggy hill and the cliffs. It is not far to drive and is well worth a visit. It is also close enough for the more energetic to make a bracing walk along the coastal path or over the fields from St Ives. The farming village has a delightful church, the Tinner's Arms and a fascinating museum. St Sennara's church has a famous carving of a mermaid on an old bench end, now part of a chair. Outside the south porch is a slate memorial to John Davey of Boswednack, said to be the last person to speak Cornish when he died in 1891. The Wayside Museum is at an old mill and has many local displays on domestic, farming, milling, mining, quarrying and smithing themes from prehistory to the mid-20th century. A footpath leads down to the dramatic cliffs of Zennor Head, while above the village are the rocky slopes of Zennor Hill. Granite is everywhere and one large block has 'W.H. Hudson often came here' carved on its face as a memorial to the naturalist and writer who stayed in the village in the early 1900s. 'Logan' or rocking stones can be found on the hill and at the south end is Zennor Quoit, a prehistoric burial chamber with a massive sloping capstone. D.H. Lawrence lived nearby during the Great War and wrote of Zennor: 'It is a most beautiful place, a tiny village nestling under high, shaggy moorhills, a big sweep of sea beyond, such lovely sea, lovelier than the Mediterranean... It is the best place I have been in.'

Knill's Steeple, Worvas Hill

Granite outcrops, the remains of an ancient hill fort and tremendous views from Trencrom Hill

NEIGHBOURHOOD WALKS

John Knill's Steeple and Steeple Woods are approached via Steeple Lane which leaves Trelyon Avenue at the Cornish Arms. The steeple stands above the woods on a high summit which provides splendid views far around. Each of the three faces of the slender granite pyramid atop John Knill's empty mausoleum is inscribed: 'Resurgam' ('I shall rise again') above his coat-of-arms on one, with 'Johannes Knill 1782' and 'I know that my redeemer liveth' on the others. The curious ceremony held here every five years is described on pages 50-51. The Steeple Woodland Project Group has established a nature reserve in Steeple Woods and restored the heath around the summit. The whole area had become overrun by rhododendrons so open woodlands and meadow areas have been created for the benefit of the public and wildlife. There is some evidence of past mining activities here.

The top of **Rosewall Hill** can be gained from a lay-by at a col 2 miles out of St Ives on the Zennor road. The two summits bristle with granite tors and boulders, and those at the eastern end, overlooking old mine workings, have at one time been called the Cuckoo Rocks. There are superb views across St Ives Bay and along the north Cornish coast to St Agnes and Trevose Heads, and the Lizard peninsula can be glimpsed on the south coast. Opposite the lay-by is the small Trevalgan Hill which has a rounded granite boulder bearing a simple memorial to the artist Peter Lanyon who died in a glider accident in 1964. These hills look down over the patchwork of tiny fields which probably date back to prehistoric times. Their boundary walls are made of granite cleared from the fields long ago and are typical of the flat strip between the hills and coast all the way to Zennor and beyond.

The **Coastal Footpath** can be followed in both directions from St Ives. A popular walk is out to the Man's Head Rock on Carrick Du at the west end of Porthmeor Beach. An easy path continues beyond to Clodgy Point which gives tantalising views of rugged cliffs and head-lands to the west. In no time at all you can escape the bustle of the town to stand or sit by the sea on lonely cliffs. The path now becomes more difficult and continues, for those who wish, to Trevalgan Point and then along a wild stretch of coast to Zennor, from which it is possible to return by footpath through the fields.

Trencrom Hill, 3 miles south of St Ives, can be reached by car or by footpaths. It was given to the National Trust in memory of the fallen of both world wars. It is a place full of atmosphere and the granite walls of an Iron Age hillfort surround its flat but rocky summit where there are traces of hut circles too. This hilltop commands the gateway to the West Penwith peninsula and overlooks the ancient land route between the Hayle estuary and Mount's Bay, a passage now followed by the A30 and main railway to Penzance. Trencrom is also one of Cornwall's great viewpoints, with both coasts and much of the county clearly seen. Emerging like islands from the planed-off landscape are the graceful forms of Godolphin and Tregonning Hills away to the south east and Carn Brea and St Agnes Beacon to the east. On a clear day the view from Trencrom is fantastic, up through Cornwall to the St Austell china clay district and the distant heights of Brown Willy and Roughtor on Bodmin Moor.

There is a tradition that the giants who dwelt here buried their gold beneath the rocks and this is now guarded by the Spriggans, evil-looking creatures of Cornish folklore. This is fanciful stuff, but the rocks are very real to see and have names such as the Giant's Chair, Cradle and Spoon, while the Giant's Well is nearby. The giants of Trencrom and St Michael's Mount are said to have played bob buttons. The buttons were flat slabs of granite placed on the Mount (the 'bob') and squarish blocks were hurled from the summit of Trencrom (the 'mit'). The giants also played bowls on Trencrom, and one rolled down the hill and was never recovered. This is the Bowl Rock, or Giant's Bowl, a lonely rounded granite boulder lying next to a cottage beside the Lelant Downs Road. It is under the care of the National Trust.

THE RAILWAY

Cornwall's most westerly branch line, just 4 miles long, was opened to St Ives from the main line at St Erth station in 1877. It has survived threats of closure and provides one of the prettiest journeys in the county. Visitors may alight from main line trains to catch the St Ives train at St Erth, or make use of the Lelant park-and-ride station nearby. After following the shore of the Hayle estuary, the railway passes the entrance channel and Hayle Bar before the scene changes to a wide vista of St Ives Bay and the open sea as the line hugs the coast. The wind was so strong that it forced a train to stop here during the 'Cintra Gale' of November 1893. There is a deep rock cutting before the train halts at the little station at Carbis Bay. Then it is away again, over a viaduct and hugging the coast close to the sea before rounding Porthminster Point through a last cutting to emerge at St Ives. Formerly, passengers arrived at the busy station overlooking Porthminster Beach, but in 1971 the sidings and the Victorian buildings were cleared to make a car park (what else?), so now the little train sidles almost unnoticed into a short platform at the back of it all. Main line excursion trains once arrived at St Ives, a far cry from the tiny railcar now shuttling back and forth on the line.

The St Ives branch line as it leaves Lelant station

Bedford Road United Methodist Church

The Bible Christian Chapel at Back Road West, one of the small Methodist chapels situated in St Ives

68

WESLEY AND ST IVES

John Wesley, the energetic evangelist and founder of Methodism, visited St Ives at least 25 times between 1743 and 1789. Indeed, St Ives was the first place he preached in Cornwall when he found a non-conformist society of nearly 100 members already established here but troubled by opposition. He first came on 30th August 1743 and stayed in the area for three weeks. On the following day there were disturbances after he had preached, when 'many began to be turbulent', but his local supporter John Nelson spoke to the loudest culprits, who went quietly away. When still in the district, Wesley preached at Sennen and Zennor, and sailed over to Scilly and returned in a St Ives fishing boat. Back in St Ives he was preaching on a Friday evening when 'Satan began to fight for his kingdom. The mob of the town burst into the room, and created much disturbance.' He returned the following spring and on 12th April he was at John Nance's house when a mob surrounded it crying 'Bring out the Preacher! Pull down the house.' They only dispersed when the mayor read the Riot Act. After this early resistance, Wesley finally become accepted and popular with most of the townsfolk.

In 1750 he still met some opposition from gentlemen while preaching near the Market Place, when a man rode his horse through the congregation. When he preached in the same place 20 years later, 'well nigh the whole town were present, and thousands from all parts of the country.' Thereafter he received a similar reception whenever he came to St Ives. John Wesley's last visit was on 25th August 1789, when he preached again at the Market Place. He wrote: 'Well nigh all the town attended, and with all possible seriousness. Surely forty years' labour has not been in vain here.' He was then aged 86 and died two years later.

The legacy of Wesley and non-conformism can be seen in the chapels about the town: Wesleyan in the Stennack (with the site of John Nance's house behind) and Bedford Road; Primitive Methodist and Congregational in Fore Street, and the Bible Christian Chapel in Back Road West.

Giew Mine, Cripplesease

MINING

The whole area around St Ives has been mined for copper and tin for centuries and even today it is not unusual to learn of mineshafts suddenly collapsing in gardens or even beneath houses! St Ives has many examples of the Cornish word 'wheal' meaning a mine working and, although most undertakings were small, they collectively employed hundreds of workers during boom times. Wheal Dream was around the site of the Museum, while ancient workings are known on The Island. The North Battery Tin Mine was opened in about 1821 on the west side of The Island and went a short way out under the sea. In 1840 part of this mine was worked as Wheal Snuff from Porthmeor Beach. Carrick Du Mine was worked for copper in the first half of the 19th century on the headland at the west end of the beach. South of here Wheal Ayr was a copper and tin mine. The Pedn Olva Hotel stands on the site of an engine house and in the cliff below is an early 19th-century mine level (adit) with a ruined granite wall built to protect it from the sea. Wheal Margery worked for tin beneath Porthminster Point from at least 1770 until 1868. At Carbis Bay, the extensive Providence Mines were at work for tin and copper from the 18th century.

The Stennack ('place of tin') valley was once busy with tin streamworks and mines. The waste tips or burrows of the old Trenwith Mine overlook the south side of Stennack valley. Although chiefly a copper mine, the old tips were worked over for about ten years from 1907 for pitchblende, an ore of uranium sought by Madame Marie Curie at the time. In 1908 Trenwith became part of St Ives Consolidated Mines, a re-working of several mines using electricity from its own power station.

St Ives Consolidated was the principal tin mine. When worked earlier as St Ives Consols it was noted for its large ore bodies known as 'carbonas', but in 1844 the workings were destroyed when timbers in the Great Carbona accidentally caught fire and burnt for six weeks. Giew Mine was also part of St Ives Consolidated Mines and has the best surviving engine house near St Ives. It is a prominent landmark beside the B3311 at Cripplesease on Frank's Shaft, which is 1,300 feet deep (or 217 fathoms as the mines were usually measured). The 'bob wall' which supported the massive beam of the steam pumping engine is dated 1874. Beyond the engine house and shaft are the foundations for the headgear, winding engine and compressor house of the 1908 re-working. This tin mine is part of the old Wheal Reeth, worked at great profit before the mid-18th century. When the St Ives Consolidated Mines went into liquidation in February 1915, work on the profitable parts of Giew continued and the mine yielded 226 tons of 'black tin' for the smelters in 1920. As tin prices fell, Giew was for a time the only tin producer in Cornwall – its greatest claim to fame – but work finally ceased in November 1922.

Looking out of one of several adits along Carbis Bay beach which drain the Providence Mines

EARLY TOURISM

'In the midst of mines, and open to a very fine bay bounded by bold rocks of black killas, stands the town of St Ives, a populous sea-port and borough' ran a description of the late 18th century. The accounts of early travellers and visitors are a wonderful source of information on the development of St Ives from a fishing village to tourist resort. Few writers declined to mention the fish and the accompanying smells and sights, so the town was not always considered such a 'quaint' fishing place as perceived today. The scene described by Walter White in the 1850s was not of a handsome town, but one appearing to be 'in a state of dilapidation, and to have been built without any regard to order. Travellers to the Mediterranean say that it reminds them of towns on the shores of Greece. Unrestrained and picturesque.' Alluding no doubt to the fishing industry and its notorious smells, White concluded: 'Do not disenchant yourself by going down into the town, but strike off the nearest way along the cliffs for Hayle.' One might almost give the same advice today at the height of the summer tourist season when the place is choked with a barely penetrable throng!

John Murray's *Handbook for Travellers in Devon and Cornwall* was written for early tourists. The 1865 edition, published a dozen years before the railway arrived, states: 'The old rickety houses of St Ives lie nestling on the very skirt of the sea, and with the blue of sky and ocean, the green tints of the shallows, and the sparkle of the bright yellow sandy shore, altogether form a very pleasing picture.' Already acknowledged as a 'gem of western scenery', St Ives was likened to a Greek village from a distance. The handbook adds that being the headquarters of the pilchard fishery, the town was 'therefore tainted with the "effluvia" of the cellars.' The Rev Francis Kilvert's diary of 1870 relates a much quoted story of the vicar of St Ives saying that the smell of the fish was so terrible that it could stop the church clock!

Now that the motor car rules our lives it is easy to forget that the growth of tourism in Cornwall, and St Ives, owes much to the Great Western Railway. By the early 20th century the GWR was promoting the 'Cornish Riviera' as a desirable place to visit by train, for family holidaymakers and those more discerning visitors seeking something different. This was really a campaign to entice passenger traffic onto their holiday lines and St Ives would have been largely passed-by if the branch line had not been opened in 1877. One wonders how differently the resort would have developed without this boost from the railway. Promotion of St Ives was achieved through publications and posters which emphasised the picturesque town, harbour, beaches and artists' colony. In 1928 the GWR published a book *The Cornish Riviera* in which the respected writer S.P.B. Mais described the town's narrow alleyways, the artists' studios and the ever-busy harbour. Industries were then evenly divided between painting and fishing, although the latter was in decline. In Mais's time the resort was already highly popular (arguably as a result of the GWR's efforts) for even then the streets were crowded almost to bursting point at the height of the season. Nevertheless, Mais wrote: 'It is easily the best centre for the extreme west of Cornwall, partly because the natives go so far out of their way to ensure their visitors' comfort. If ever there was a place where one feels instantly at home it is St Ives.'

Three quarters of a century later, many may recognise these sentiments today, yet however much the town and its people have changed over the years, the setting of St Ives – the sea and the magnificent cliff scenery - remains as glorious as ever.

The kind of views and light which brought early tourists to the town and attracted the artists who founded the St Ives School

St Ives harbour and harbour front

The St Ives area offers visitors and locals alike spectacular views

St Ives and the surrounding area not only provides attractive surroundings but also wonderful natural sporting venues. Above: a kite surfer enjoys an evening's surfing at Porthmeor Beach (Photo: Richard Clegg). The coastline and granite outcrops of the area provide some excellent bouldering and rock climbing (bottom left). More traditional sports are also popular with St Ives boasting its own rugby, football, hockey, netball, Surf Life Saving and sailing clubs (bottom right) among others

Porthmeor beach is renowned for its surf and surfers of all kinds, from long boarders to bodyboarders, are regularly out enjoying the waves. Surf kayaks and Surf Skis are also common sights around St Ives

Positioned as it is, St Ives is sometimes subject to the full force of Atlantic gales which can provide some spectacular scenes during the winter months

Photo: Tony Smith

SOME FURTHER READING

St Ives Port & Harbour - A Short History;
Bret Guthrie priced £3.99. ISBN 0 948385 19 7.

Downlong Days - A St Ives Miscellany;
Eddie Murt priced £9.90. ISBN 0 948385 17 0.

Extracts from The St Ives Weekly Summary 1889-1910;
Joyce Channon priced £5.40. ISBN 0 948385 07 3.

20 Short Walks Around St Ives;
Margaret Sharp priced £2.99. ISBN 0 948385 12 X.

C. Gull - His Point of View, (a cartoon look at St Ives' seagulls);
Zan Dyer priced £1.00. ISBN 0 948385 18 9.

The St. Ives Times & Echo;
the independent local newspaper for the town, published every Friday.
On sale throughout the town and district.

For a full list of publications available through the local newspaper
telephone 01736 795813.

Or call in and browse;

St Ives Times & Echo, High Street (rear of HSBC Bank),
St. Ives, TR26 1RS, Cornwall.

INDEX

The National Coastwatch Institution lookout, The Island, formally an HM Coastguard lookout, the volunteers of the NCI now man the station